For my dear bro

a true Cornishm

of the Cornish ;

Love. Fred Christmas 2001.

The Cornish Pasty

C000259020

This delightful painting, called 'The Noonday Rest', is by the Cornish artist Edward Opie. Recently restored, the painting (c1850) shows a family enjoying a pasty picnic by the seaside. The setting is likely to be the St Agnes area in North Cornwall, where the artist worked. Edward Opie was the nephew of John Opie, who was hailed as 'the Cornish Wonder' and whose paintings were exhibited at the Royal Academy in the late 18th century. (Reproduced by kind permission of Mr Viv Hendra).

The Cornish Pasty

Stephen Hall

AGRE

First published in 2001 by:

AGRE BOOKS
Groom's Cottage, Nettlecombe,
Bridport, Dorset, DT6 3SS
www.agrebooks.co.uk

All rights reserved. No part of this book may be
reproduced in any form or by any means without
permission in writing from the publisher, except by a
reviewer who may quote brief passages in a review.

Copyright © 2001 Stephen Hall.
The author has asserted his moral rights.

'The Noonday Rest' copyright © 2001 Viv Hendra.

Typeset by Agre Books.
Printed and bound in Cornwall
by R. Booth Ltd, Mabe, Penryn.

ISBN 0 9538000 4 0

A CIP catalogue record for this book
is available from the British Library.

CONTENTS

'A Cornish Pasty, I'm running 'Im In'. Edwardian postcard.

Pasty Pioneers

When I view my Country o'er:
Of goodly things the plenteous store:
The Sea and Fish that swim therein
And underground the Copper and Tin:
Let all the World say what it can
Still I hold by the Cornishman,
And that one most especially
That first found out the Cornish Pastie

('The Merry Ballad of the Cornish Pasty', Robert Morton Nance, 1898)

THE pasty was the answer to every 19th century Cornish miner's prayer. It had been waiting in the wings for hundreds of years; a solution in search of a problem; an invention yearning for an application. Here at last was a highly portable, nutritious food source that, like Cornishman Humphry Davy's miner's safety lamp, promised to be an indispensable underground companion.

The pasty had graced the table of many a lord and lady in its colourful past but somehow the mutton and claret or venison with wild duck sauce versions had never quite caught on in Cornish mining circles. Cornish farm labourers had been conducting vigorous 'field trials' on pasties for decades (albeit mostly vegetarian ones) - but these were mere agricultural prototypes, not designed or built to withstand the rigours of life underground. No, if a Cornish miner was going to carry his pasty to work, then it had to meet certain criteria. These were as follows:

It should be shaped and sized to match the dimensions of a miner's pocket.

Its pastry case should be strong enough to withstand dropping down a mineshaft.

It should have sufficient insulation properties to keep its contents warm.

It should have a strong, disposable, thick handle.

It should have a partition to separate savoury and sweet contents.

It should have space in the corner for a miner's initials.

Had this been the design brief back in the early 1800s, there would have been no shortage of talented Cornish engineers ready to tackle the 'Pasty Project'. Cornwall was at the forefront of industrial innovation; it pioneered deep mining techniques that set the standard throughout the world.

Sadly, the truth is far more prosaic. There was no Pasty Project and the marriage of pasties and mining owed more to fate and co-incidence than clever arrangement. Demand for the pasty escalated when Cornish tin and copper mines flourished in the first half of the 19th century. Tens of thousands of people were employed in the industry - above and below ground - and the pasty was the staple diet of many workers. It was eminently suitable. It had a thick shortcrust pastry with strong insulation properties. Pocket-sized and pocket shaped, it could be taken anywhere. It was filled with wholesome and sustaining ingredients like beef, potatoes, onion and turnip. Some miners' wives even incorporated a sweet course at one end of the pasty - filling it with apple, jam or treacle. Unlike the pasties of earlier times however, there was no intermingling of flavours; savoury and sweet contents were separated by an internal pastry partition.

Workers in Cornwall rarely did just one job. Many miners would have sweated as agricultural labourers and vice versa. Even the humblest pasties helped to keep them going. A writer for the *St James Chronicle* observed in 1776:

For the lowest sort of people, living is so wretched that our poor in the environs of London would soon perish if reduced to their condition. The labourers in general bring up their families with only potatoes or turnips, or leeks or pepper grass, rolled up in black barley crust, and baked under the ashes, with now and then a little milk. Perhaps they do not taste a bit of flesh-meat in three months. Yet their children are healthy and strong and look quite fresh and jolly.

By the early 19th century meat was less of a rarity. G.B. Worgan, in his *Agricultural Survey of Cornwall* (1811), wrote:

Many of the labourers [...] who gain better wages, or who are not burthened with large families, use wheaten bread, and are able to indulge in some meat for their pasties, as well as for their suppers, after their daily labour is done. They have an advantage also, from the great plenty of fish with which the markets abound. Indeed, the poor are in general better fed and clothed than in most counties.

Miners who wanted food during their daily labours had to take provisions with them at the start of their shifts. Easier said than done, when going to work meant descending into the bowels of the earth via a long series of ladders, and sometimes walking far out under the sea. Tinners toiled in cramped, poorly ventilated conditions. Their punishing underground regime was not designed to let them 'pop up top' for a hot lunch or dinner. So a nutritious pasty really was ideal. It could be kept warm in a miner's breast pocket, or heated underground over a small fire on a shovel. A practice, incidentally, which could have only occurred in hard rock mines like Cornwall's, where there was no danger of explosive gasses.

In 1842 Dr Charles Burham produced a report for the Royal Commission on Children's Employment in Cornish mines. It gives a fascinating insight into the conditions above and below ground:

Every miner now takes some sort of food with him when he goes underground - an innovation on the custom 20 or 30 years ago, which has justly been considered most beneficial. Their pasties or hoggans are the most usual articles of this kind.

The hoggan was a distant cousin of the pasty - known in the 18th century as 'a lump of unleavened dough, in which was sometimes embedded a morsel of green [unsmoked] pork'. The word 'hoggan' was also used to describe a bag in which miners carried their meals. It is the likely source for 'oggy' or 'oggie' - a slang term for the pasty in some parts of the South West.

Dr Burham found there was little in the way of comfort or mixing of the sexes at meal times. Younger boys would eat their pasties 'almost by snatches' and spend the rest of the time playing games. At Trethellan Copper Mine near Redruth he noted:

The boys and girls chiefly have potato pasties, with some of them a little meat, mostly pork in them; hoggans are not so plenty as they used to be. There is in most cases as much as they can get... The word 'hoggan', called in different districts 'hobban' and 'fuggan', is a coarse kind of cake, prepared by incorporating pieces of potato, or sometimes raisins, with a sheet of dough, which was then rolled up and baked.

Despite its basic contents, the sustaining value of the miners' hoggan is vividly expressed in a song written in 1900 by Herbert Thomas, the editor of *The Cornishman* newspaper in Penzance:

Aw, you don't want fancy denners when you're sweaten bare your bones,
   An' feel as ef you could digest a barraful of stones,
'Tes for somethin' braave and solid that you know your sperit groans,
   And a hoggan like stull tember you could chew comrade.

As the food of the common man the pasty nourished a new vocabulary. There were at least three different words for lunch in Cornwall: 'crowst' (or 'croust'), 'crib' or 'snap'. It is thought that crowst derives from the crust on the edge of a pasty, which is also known as a 'crimp'. The art of 'crimping' is discussed later.

'Crib' may well come from being 'cribbed' - meaning confined; either because the miners were confined underground or that their food was confined in the pastry, or both. It could also relate to the practice of making vent holes in the pasty to prevent bursting when heated (from the Latin 'cribum' meaning 'marked like a sieve') or it may be a corruption of crimped. 'Snap' probably refers to the issue of tins with tight seals to miners. The tins were closed by two spring-loaded catches which snapped open and shut to seal the contents.

The time and facilities children were allowed for crowst seems to have varied from mine to mine. On his visit to Consolidated Mines near Truro in May 1841, Dr Burham observed: 'No time is allowed for crowst, but at about nine or ten they take a bit of pasty when the agent is not looking, holding it in one hand and working with the other.' At Carnon Consols Mine near Redruth, conditions were vastly improved:

They have the use of a couple of small houses to eat their dinners in, and there is an oven connected with the furnace for them to warm their pasties... I have observed their pasties; they are usually well provided with meat; the hoggans are comparatively rare.

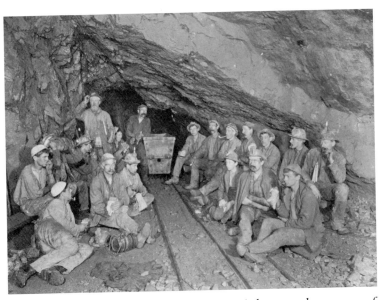

Croust time East Pool Mine, Illogan, 1893. (Photograph courtesy of the Royal Institution of Cornwall Photographic Collection.)

The provision of ovens and eating areas was also uncommon. At Fowey Consols there was a long iron cylinder heated at one end by a fire. This was used to warm the shed in which meals were taken, and to heat up pasties. Workers who wanted their pasties even hotter could have them warmed in communal ovens known as bakehouses at a charge of one penny a week. At some mines pasties were heated on the steam boilers by the 'bal maidens' - women who broke up the ore with hammers. In places where ore was smelted, pasties were kept warm on cooling blocks of tin. At the end of the 19th century, a resourceful woman in Camborne operated a popular pasty delivery service for miners.

She drove around the area in a donkey cart each morning. Every few yards she blew a whistle and housewives brought out pasties, each in a named bag, which she delivered to the mines nearby.

Arguably, it was the pasty's crimp that really set it apart as the miner's friend. The crimp became a handle that could be thrown away by the miner once the pasty had been consumed. The theory is that this reduced the chances of him being poisoned - as arsenic was frequently present in tin mines. However, as with pasties themselves, there is more than one side to the story and some people hotly dispute that miners would have been so wasteful. More likely, they contend, workers would have been able to wash their hands and/or would have wrapped the pasty in a bag or cloth, then eaten it from corner to corner. Certainly, photographs of 19th century miners do appear to show them eating pasties in some sort of wrapper - supporting the latter view. A napkin is referred to in this extract from Robert Morton Nance's 'The Merry Ballad of the Cornish Pasty' (1898):

When the Tinner to Bal takes a touchpipe for crowse
He cannot have Hot Meat sent from his house:
Yet hath no stomach for victuals cold
So a Pasty he takes in a Napkin rolled:
And though he leave it for half the day
Within his Hoggan Bag warm 'twill stay
So I wish him joy, whoever he be
That first found out the Cornish Pastie

Pasties provided a man-sized meal for hungry Cornishmen.

CROUST TIME

"This is our denner."

Father like mate and tatie best
Mother like turmut and mate
Boy Jack want 'all mate
Boy Tom like lickey best
an' the maidens edden pertic'lar' tall.

A work pasty would often be marked with the owner's initials added to the left or right hand side with a strip of pastry. This practice was also useful in large households if you wanted to save a corner to eat later. Not everyone liked turnip and there's a well-known Cornish story about a woman who put the initials 'TT' in the corner of all her pasties. At dinner time she dished them out as 'tis turmut' to some of her family and 'tidn't turmut' to the others.

By the 1860s it was clear that Cornish people had taken the pasty to their hearts, and that it was being mass produced in many succulent forms in mining towns and villages.

The young people employed above ground, usually work ten hours a day in summer, and nine in winter. Their wages are paid smoothly and vary from three or four pence a day, to four or five shillings a week. They usually dine at the mines, and like the other mining operatives, carry their dinners to the mines in what they call croust bags. These bags seldom contain anything but pasties, which, by-the-bye, are quite an institution in Cornwall. A stranger taking a morning's stroll through one of the mining villages, should be almost certain to have his attention arrested by the numerous pasties that were being carried to, or from, the public bakehouses. And were he to enter one of those establishments, he might be shown such a bill of pasty-fare, that for variety at least, would vie with those usually laid on the tables of first class hotels. He might feast in imagination, if not in fact, on bacon pasties, fish pasties, beef pasties, potato pasties, turnip pasties, mutton pasties, leek pasties and pasties made of almost everything else that can be eaten and digested.

WICH'E WILL'E' AVE? A TURMUT, TATEY OR LICKEY PASTY?

Writing in 1869, the Reverend Charles Garton Honor was clearly dazzled by the variety of pasties available, although he apparently resisted the temptation to try one himself. It is interesting to note that at no point does he refer to the 'Cornish' pasty. The prefix crept into more common usage in late Victorian and Edwardian times with the growth of tourism, railways and faster systems of communication. The term 'Cornish pasty' came to be used by visitors and those outside the county, whereas Cornish people have always referred to their national dish simply as a 'pasty'.

In the early 1900s postcards provided a cheap, reliable and rapid means of communication. Cornish photographers and printers were quick to exploit the new medium. Alongside rural and seaside views, dozens of postcards were produced depicting the pasty (often humorously) as a symbol of Cornwall. These

'I would as soon 'ave a good old pasty and a dish 'o tay for my denner as onything'.

ABOVE AND OPPOSITE: *Two views of a tasty Cornish tea as depicted on postcards from the early 20th century.*

images have now become sought-after collectors' items. Good copies can command high prices, especially the colour tinted versions. In preparing this book, I was fortunate to be offered specimens from the collections of Paddy Bradley, Gerald Luke and Clive Benney.

By the early 20th century, the pasty had become synonymous with the county. Every home and every bakehouse churned out pasties to feed hungry miners or farm workers. But the demand for pasties could not have been met without the invention of the Cornish range, a solid fuel stove which revolutionised the Duchy's domestic life.

Pasty Pride

RIGHT up until the 1930s it was common in rural parts of Cornwall to cook on an open fire of peat. Many Cornish kitchens had an inglenook with a flat hearth raised about a foot above floor level. A fire would be built on this platform, using peat from local sources. Cut-up turf or even dried cowpats would be set alight, then an iron plate, often called an 'under baker' or a 'flat-ire', would be placed above the flames. Once the under baker had heated up, a pasty would go on top of that, then it would be covered with a baking iron or 'bake-ire' - a shallow cover which had to be surrounded with more peat. Enterprising cooks could tell whether or not a pasty was cooked by holding up a glass to the bake-ire and listening to the pasty hissing inside. But cooking by these methods was far from an exact science, as a visitor to Cornwall (writing for the Edinburgh-based *Chambers Journal*) pointed out in 1900:

The fire was... raked around, and it rested with the cook to settle in her own mind, as by a sort of clairvoyance, at what moment the operation had been completed. In these days a good deal of wrong-doing may be wrought by the cook who does not know how to manage her oven, or neglects to watch it; but imagine what opportunities of disaster surrounded the woman who had to make use of 'baker' and baking iron!

Another possibility was the eathenware cloam oven, set into an open chimney. The cloam was shaped like a tall dome (about

18 x 18 inches). It had a detachable oven door, and many sported a distinctive crow's foot mark on top - to keep the devil away from the hearth, a sacred and holy place. The oven was heated by burning bundles of sticks or furze inside it. The temperature was tested by rubbing a broom handle on the earthenware - if it sparked it was hot enough! Pasties would then be placed inside

A typical 19th century cloam oven.

and the cloam door sealed with river mud or clay. The residual heat in the oven baked the pasties, which were removed by chipping the door out. Manufacturing cloam ovens took considerable skill. Many were made at Lakes Pottery in Truro until 1937. To render them fireproof, Lakes' ovens were tempered with quartz crystals, as opposed to the coarse gravels used for oven-making by North Devon potters. Lakes also produced a wide range of cooking utensils for Cornwall's farming and fishing communities, including tall pans called 'bussas' in which pilchards were salted down for preservation.

The invention of the solid-fuel stove in the 1840s revolutionised domestic life in the county. For the first time, women had full control over their baking. With a Cornish Range, or 'slab' as it

The Cornish Cooking Range.

THE MOST SIMPLE, ECONOMICAL AND EFFECTIVE RANGE MADE.

Nothing to get out of order.

Effective Damper for checking draught.

Perfect Combustion of fuel.

Oven takes out for cleaning purposes and put back with the greatest ease.

3-FOOT RANGE WITH CAST COVINGS AND JAMBS AS SUPPLIED TO THE HON. TRINITY CORPORATION FOR LIGHTHOUSE SHORE-DWELLINGS THROUGHOUT THE KINGDOM.

MAKERS: N. HOLMAN & SONS, Ltd., St. JUST.

PRICES AT BACK.

was known, pasties could be browned to perfection. If the fire was turned down to the correct level, the flavours could all soak through. The first Cornish ranges were made by N. Holman & Sons, an engineering company based at St Just in the west of Cornwall. Demand for these ranges soared - despite their hefty £4 price tag. Most slabs were plain and small with a brass doorknob and drying rack. Much more expensive were the highly ornamented and panelled versions that graced big farmhouses or Victorian villas. Cornish Ranges were exported worldwide, especially to countries where Cornish miners emigrated. Holman's even designed a range for fishing boats and as early as 1862 they made one for the Seven Stones Light Vessel, moored off the Cornish coast.

With the growing popularity of the slab, the kitchen became

the heart of the home. Here it was the brightest, busiest and warmest (few families enjoyed the luxury of heating upstairs). Children witnessed cooking activities from a very early age. Writing in 1949, Cornish author and broadcaster Claude Berry recalled a vivid kitchen scene:

When I was growing up, I liked to watch mother rolling out the pastry until it was about a quarter of an inch thick, then putting a plate on it and cutting round the edge, so that she had as many circles of pastry as she intended to make pasties. Half the circle would be laid over a rolling pin, while the beef, potatoes, turnip and onion, cut into small pieces, were placed on the other half. Then the edges of the pastry were damped and the filling was enclosed between the two semi-circles. With forefingers and thumb mother would neatly crimp the edges - so there was always a wavy effect - and make a slit in the top to let the steam out. Into a quick oven the four or five pasties would go and in about three-quarters of an hour out they came, smelling as good as they looked.

So there you have it. A simple, no-nonsense account of how to make a Cornish pasty - except that no two households in a single Cornish street are likely to do the same. Some may use skirt or chuck steak, some may add liver to improve the gravy, some may use margarine or suet or dripping as well as lard in making the pastry, and some may use more seasoning than others. Even when you've decided on the ingredients for your perfect pasty, there are several other important issues to be addressed. Should the vegetables be sliced or diced? Should the pastry be glazed or un-glazed? And perhaps the most burning issue of all - should the pasty be crimped on the side or on top? The consensus is that vegetables should be sliced and not cubed. Similarly meat must be cut and never minced and always cooked from raw:

There is perhaps only one substance which has never been used in the manufacture of a genuine article of the kind, and that is minced meat. One does not know why, but it has never been used. By some curious freak of chance it is a substance upon which the cook who is not Cornish blunders almost inevitably when she sets forth to demonstrate that anybody who has the least culinary knowledge can make a pasty. (*Chambers Journal*, 1900)

Glazing is a matter of personal preference. It is usually done with egg or milk, but should you be thinking of entering your pasty in a competition, it's probably wise to seek the judges' opinion beforehand!

Most of all though, Cornwall is a divided county on the question of top or side crimping. Photographs of 19th century miners or farm workers show many eating pasties crimped on the side. In *Cornish Recipes - Ancient and Modern* produced by the Women's Institute in 1929, pasty producers are recommended to 'fold the pastry over into a semi-circle' and to 'shape the pasty nicely and crimp the extreme edges where it is joined between finger and thumb'. Furthermore, the WI's advice on 'how to eat a pasty' seems to lean towards side-crimping:

When the pasties are being made, each member of the family has his or hers marked at one corner with the initial of the prospective owner. In this way, each person's tastes can be catered for. The true Cornish way to eat a pasty is to hold it in the hand, and begin to bite it from opposite end to the initial, so that, should any of it be uneaten, it may be consumed later by its rightful owner. And woe betide anyone who takes another person's corner!

However, top-crimpers argue their method is more scientific and makes for a tastier pasty. A more oval shape, they contend, holds the gravy better. The potato, when thinly sliced, forms top and bottom layers, while the meat and other vegetables in between help to make the steam that creates the gravy, which in this layered fashion is distributed more evenly. There is one way out of this side-versus-top crimp dilemma - and that is to choose neither. Instead, you could follow the example of some commercial bakers and create a pasty with a slightly offset crimp - midway between a side and top crimp.

Just as opinion is divided over crimping, so too there are split views on whether pasties should contain savoury and sweet ingredients. Such toothsome twosomes are said to have been popular with miners and farm workers - but very few recipes exist. In her book *Cornish Cookery*, Vida Heard describes one called Farmers' Favourite: 'An extra long pasty filled with seasoned meat one end and sugared apples or jam at the other. A partition to separate the two course of the meal was achieved by making a little roll of pastry between the meat and the fruit.' Weighing against the 'dinner and pudding' pasty is the argument that even with a partition, there is the potential for the gravy or savoury juices to seep through into the sweet compartment. Also, jam and fruit cook in different timescales to meat and vegetables.

A more common approach is to make a separate sweet pasty in addition to a savoury one. A 'windy' pasty is an empty case, baked in a hot oven, then split open and eaten with jam, hot or cold. An apple pasty was a particular favourite for Anne Treneer. Her book *Schoolhouse in the Wind* gives a vivid account of her childhood in the village of Gorran in mid-Cornwall at the beginning of the 20th century:

We must have eaten various foods on Hemmick beach, since we stayed there from morn till night, but the food I best remember is apple pasties. Each child had a whole apply pasty to himself with an initial cut into the pastry before it was baked; A for Anne, S for Susan, W for Wilfrid and so on. On either side of the initial a round piece of pastry was cut out, brown sugar and Cornish cream inserted and the pieces of pastry put back. Sometimes we lifted these lids and licked the cream and sugar first, but the right way to eat a pasty is to hold it upright in both hands and begin at the top corner, biting on and on through mediocre and delicious alike to the last crumb of the bottom corner.

A dollop of cream, or 'raw-ream', also added a finishing touch to some savoury pasties. Ones made with the very first vegetables of the season - e.g. turnip pasty, new potato pasty, broccoli pasty - would be baked very quickly and dressed with a spoonful of cream when taken out of the oven.

Pasty contests are a regular event at local agricultural and horticultural shows. Each year, a battalion of highly-trained Women's Institute judges swings into action - deployed throughout the county to scrutinise entries and award prizes only for the very best pasties. The WI ladies have strict judging criteria: first, the outside appearance of the pasty is closely examined; then it is picked up to assess its hand-holding qualities; then it is cut in half and the volume and distribution of its contents inspected and, finally and mostly importantly, it is tasted for flavour. There are men's and women's competitions. Females prefer pasties of six to eight inches in length, while men, it seems, like to offer up a good nine inches or more. But it is ultimately flavour, not size, that matters most.

It is a sin to put peas or carrots into a traditional beef pasty but just about anything else qualifies - chicken, pork, rabbit, bacon, egg, mackerel, apple, jam or dates. Lily May's father worked as a stableman at Lanhydrock House near Bodmin in the 1900s. She recalls a delightful tale about pasties in 'Recollections of Lanhydrock' (*Cornish Life*, 1985):

We could tell everyone's pasties at school. Some were beef and potatoes; some were egg and bacon; some were apple. The trappers used to catch rabbits and their children had rabbit pasties. There were 'pasty girls' chosen for a week at school. They had to warm the pasties beside the classroom fire at 11 am to be ready for 12.00. If we had special friends, we would put them in the best place to get warm. If they weren't so popular we would put them at the back where they didn't get so warm.

The cosy picture conjured up in that school contrasts sharply with a report in 1912 by Dr Barnes, County Medical Officer of Health. His investigation into the diets of schoolchildren makes disturbing reading:

Malnutrition constitutes one of the worst physical disabilities of the schoolchild; it is closely associated with many of the defects found. Fortunately in Cornwall the number of really necessitous children is small and the great bulk of the cases which must necessarily be placed in this category arise mainly through ignorance of the best methods of preparing and administering food.

The Cornish pasty, which constitutes so frequently the main meal of the scholar, is frequently made of indigestible pastry and packed with ill-cooked vegetables, chiefly potatoes, which are not only supply an excessive quantity of starchy material, so detrimental to the teeth, but must lie heavily in the stomach, since they are cold, and consequently hard, when eaten. Possibly the enormous amount of dental caries is contributed to in this manner; practically 41% of the children examined had evidence of some bad teeth and how many more would have been discovered by a careful dentist with his probe and mirror?

There is associated with this vast problem of nutrition the important subject of cookery instruction and opportunities for heating dinners in our schools. The former is happily being taken in hand by the Education Authority, with great hope for the future, but the latter requires the serious consideration of school managers in many parts of the county.

Doan't 'ee say no when you'm
axed to 'ave a Pasty (68)

Doubtless Dr Barnes would not have approved of the favoured drink with pasties - very sweet tea. Traditionally, many Cornish people of strong Methodist stock didn't have sugar because John Wesley used to preach against the slave trade and demanded a boycott of sugar. But somehow a special sugar-in-tea concession seems to have been granted when it came to pasties...

And, even at the dinner table, the tradition of eating pasties hand-held is still the required Cornish convention. Pasties are best consumed straight from the oven, wrapped in a paper bag. Often made to individual taste (e.g. with onion or without), pasties today are still marked in one corner with the appropriate initial.

Father like mate and tatie best,	(*meat and potato*)
Mother like turmut and mate.	(*turnip*)
Boy Jack want all mate,	
Boy Tom like lickey best,	(*leek*)
An' the maidens edden pertic'lar 'tall.	(*aren't at all particular*)

(Traditional Cornish rhyme)

Pasty Parables

THERE is no shortage of legends and superstitions about the Cornish pasty which, like many recipes, have been handed down over decades. Well-stirred and heavily seasoned these stories are part of Cornish folklore and add considerably to the pasty's charm and romance.

It's said you can put anything into a pasty - except the Devil. Legend has it that, centuries ago, the Devil was crossing one of the bridges over the River Tamar (which divides Devon and Cornwall). He looked inside a cottage window and saw a woman preparing a pasty with a set of ingredients on the table. Peering into a second cottage he saw another woman with another set of ingredients. When the Devil came across a third woman and asked, 'What actually goes into a Cornish pasty?' the woman picked up a cleaver and said 'You next, my son!'

The Devil promptly hightailed it back into Devon and has never crossed the Tamar into Cornwall again - because Cornish women will put anything into a pasty!

Doubtless, Cornwall's reputation as the 'land of saints' would have added to the Devil's reluctance to venture over the border, as the author of *England in the 19th Century* observed in 1842:

The Devil will not venture among the Cornish, for fear of being sainted or put in a pie; the variety of sainted churches as of pies being pretty nearly equal, and some of them both excellent in their way.

Many Cornish fishermen are highly superstitious about taking a pasty to sea with them - however much they may like eating them ashore. As a taboo, carrying a pasty onto a boat ranks as highly in fishermen's bad-luck stakes as mentioning white hares or meeting a clergyman while on the way to a boat. Some believe that even speaking of pasties and boats is a 'cold iron' - meaning that the guilty person should touch a piece of cold iron (rather like touching wood) to ward off ill luck or evil spirits.

Cadgwith fishermen on the Lizard found one way of overcoming the superstition. If they discovered someone had brought a pasty on board, they would break off the ends - allowing the wind to blow through it and the Devil to escape!

For some fishing folk however, thoughts of evil spirits or ill-fortune were put aside and the pasty made a trusty companion. Witness this from *The Merry Ballad of the Cornish Pasty*:

And when the Fisher a fishing goes
Though rough winds redden his ears and nose
Little he careth how hard it blow
So his pasty lie safe in the locker below
For though the lugger should ship a sea
Within its crust still dry 'twould be
So I wish him joy, whoever he be
That first found out the Cornish Pastie.

In common with other cultures, Cornwall has many stories about its 'little people'. According to folklore, early Stone Age and Bronze Age settlements produced an alienated tribe of Cornish imps or goblins called 'Buccas'. Banished to impenetrable moors, forests and even subterranean worlds they were rarely and fleetingly glimpsed. Underground Buccas were also known as 'knackers' or 'knockers' - ugly sprites said to be suffering perpetual penance. As miners plumbed ever greater depths in the quest for tin or copper, Buccas would knock on the side of the mine wall to warn of the imminent danger of a fall. Technically, this effect was probably due to the crystalline structure of tin ore; the cracking of crystal plates does cause a knocking sound. Nevertheless, the miners of old took no chances, and to stay on the right side of the knockers, they would leave a portion of their pasty as a peace offering. Not, presumably, the arsenic-contaminated crimp, as the little creatures were very temperamental. Properly treated, Buccas could be friendly and helpful, leading a miner towards rich mineral veins or guiding him away from danger. But once wronged or neglected, they could be vindictive enemies. There is a well-known story of Tom Trevorrow, a miner who fell foul of the Buccas in just this way. Stopping to eat his fuggan (Cornish heavycake), he heard the eerie singing:

Tom Trevorrow! Tom Trevorrow !
Leave some of thy fuggan for bucca
Or bad luck to thee to-morrow!

Tom unwisely ignored this warning and ate every last morsel of his fuggan. The Buccas then cast their evil spell:

Tommy Trevorrow! Tommy Trevorrow!
We'll send thee bad luck tomorrow;
Thou old curmudgeon to eat all thy fuggan,
And not leave a didjan for bucca.

(Traditional)

Tom's luck ran out at this point and thereafter his life was dogged with ill-fortune; so much so that he had to quit mining to find work on the land.

One of the secrets of a successful pasty is its pastry. Miners are supposed to prefer a pasty that's so robust their wives could drop it from the top of a mineshaft and they could catch it - intact - at the bottom. The story's told that one man married a cook from a well-to-do family and she made him some pasties that were deliciously light. But when she asked her husband if he had enjoyed his pasty, he replied: 'A wadn'no good at all. Time

I got to fifty fathoms a were scattered to lembs [broken to bits]. The wans mawther made wadn' break if they'd faaled to the bottom of the shaft. They *was* pasties, you!'

Then there is the link between rodents and pasties. Perhaps this is where the phrase 'rat's coffin' comes from - a less endearing term for Cornwall's most famous food, doubtless emanating from east of the Tamar. In the 19th century children were threatened with 'mousey pasties' if they wet their beds - a threat that was supposed to cure this problem!

Matthew, Mark, Luke and John
Ate a pasty five foot long
Ate it once and ate it twice
Oh my Lord, it's full of mice.
(*Traditional*)

It is fabled that St George's Island, also known as Looe Island in South East Cornwall, was once infested with rats. The inhabitants took a vow to eat nothing but rat pasty until they had rid themselves of the rodents. The rats didn't last very last long, apparently.

Some people subscribe to the view that many modern marriage breakdowns could be avoided if more attention was paid to the pre-marital pasty than pre-marital sex. While physical attractions might wane over a period of time, a Cornish maid's pasty-making abilities will sustain her for a lifetime.

Pasties a-plenty

THREE million pasties are produced in Cornwall every week - enough to stretch four times across the county from Land's End to Bude. Ninety per cent of them are sold outside the county. The industry has an annual turnover of £150 million and provides thousands of jobs. A product which evolved from a humble agricultural and mining past is now a cornerstone of the Cornish economy. But how are these pasties made? Who buys them and what goes into them?

Many people argue that home-baked pasties are - and always will be - vastly superior to their commercial counterparts. 'The ones that mother makes are the best pasties' is a frequently heard comment in Cornwall. Bakers strive hard to reproduce that elusive but precious home-baked quality - often with impressive results. But under current EU regulations, the Cornish pasty is simply classed as a 'meat pie'. That gives producers carte blanche to determine its composition and quality - and not just in Cornwall. At one end of the scale they make pasties along strict, traditional lines using locally sourced ingredients where possible, and hand-crimpers. At the other end of the industry there are less scrupulous manufacturers. The worst are said to make 'pull-through pasties', where the dough is rolled out, some onion and potato is added, then a small piece of meat is pulled rapidly through the pastry case, leaving a slight flavour behind.

In Cornwall, scores of corner-shop bakeries churn out freshly baked pasties by the thousand, and in summer by the ten thousand in order to satisfy hungry holidaymakers starved of the real thing for the rest of the year. You don't have to search hard for a pasty shop - your nose will lead you to one. The smell of beef, potatoes, turnip, onion and pastry gently baking to perfection permeates the air in Cornish towns and villages. If the aroma could be bottled, it would top every visitor's souvenir list.

Inside a typical small bakery, half a dozen or so workers busily prepare pasties in the early hours. Pastry, rolled out of a machine, is cut into circular shapes, which are then laid out sixteen in a row on a long table. The traditional Cornish pasty mix of potatoes, turnip, onion and seasoning is measured out using a cup, then topped with beef (usually chuck steak). The pasties are crimped by hand - an experienced worker is expected to churn out sixteen pasties in as many minutes. Trayfuls of pasties are then baked in the same ovens used to make bread and sold over the counter that same morning.

The biggest player in the industry is Ginsters, based in Callington in South East Cornwall. The business was founded in 1968 by former dairy farmer Geoffrey Ginster and his two sons Gerald and Barry. Ginsters' early pasties were made in an old egg-packing station. Initially they were sold to pubs, clubs, and corner shops in Plymouth and seaside resorts. To develop a year-round market the company established depots in Winchester, London and Bristol. Big contracts were secured with hospitals, colleges, British Rail, and supermarket chains. A major outlet in the early Eighties was the armed forces' NAAFI stores. Ginsters' staff worked hard during the Falklands War to supply British troops with pasties and pies. Today the company is one of the biggest commercial employers in Cornwall, with 1,000 staff and an annual turnover of £80 million. 'Food on the move' has been one of Ginsters' major marketing slogans - many pasties are sold from garage forecourts and corner shops. More recently, Ginsters has tried to refine its 'mass-produced' image with a more upmarket, organic Cornish pasty containing organically-grown potato, swede and onion, slowly matured organic beef with organic seasonings, wrapped in a light puff pastry.

Other major producers include Warrens (one of the oldest bakeries in Cornwall, founded in 1860), W.C. Rowe, Blewetts, Proper Cornish, Crantock Bakery and Barnecutt. Crantock Bakery operates from a gleaming, purpose-built factory on an industrial estate near Newquay. The firm produces around 150,000 pasties a week, all of which are hand-crimped. In 1996 Crantock made history by becoming the first bakery to export Cornish-made pasties to the USA. It was a bold move - not least because the BSE crisis flared up right at the time of the launch in Salt Lake City, Utah. Crantock's American adventure was the subject of several television news reports and the focal point of a half-hour documentary called *Pasties Away!* I made for BBC South West in 1996. We followed the progress of Frank and Tess Bradshaw, Crantock's founders, as they unveiled their wares at a trade fair in Salt Lake City. The Americans took a great interest in the pasty - but Lady Thatcher, who was guest of honour, was less fascinated and declined an offer to taste one.

Crantock's specialises in frozen un-baked Cornish pasties for the 'bake-off' market. As well as supplying wholesalers and major retailers, the firm runs its own chain of franchised Oggy,

Oggy, Pasty shops. However, like many bakeries, Crantock has struggled to find good hand-crimpers. Its factory workers have to crimp five pasties a minute on a shift that starts at 7am and finishes at 3.30pm. The crimping craft, which years ago might

have been learned at 'mother's elbow', is a dying art. Only half the people who apply for a crimping job have the necessary skill. The rest are given training and start work on the slowest part of the production line until they are up to speed.

In the past, trainee crimpers used to learn with Plasticine, but now they are given real pastry to hone their skills.

Hand-crimping is still the method favoured by most Cornish bakeries. It's a sign of quality, performed to emulate home-made pasties. Being labour-intensive, it can add twenty per cent to a pasty's price and only very high volume producers have invested in automation. Ginsters, which manufactures around a million pasties a week, has a special machine that shapes the pastry then crimps and cuts it. Up to ten thousand pasties an hour roll off the production lines. Commercial producers not only make beef pasties. They turn out countless other versions including pork, cheese, lamb, spicy chicken and even curry. Always on the lookout for new varieties, pasty makers are rarely accused of having a head-in-the-sand attitude; in 1996 an enterprising butcher from St Austell proved a hit with his customers by producing ostrich pasties.

Across the border in Devon, Ivor Dewdney has five stores selling a million pasties a year from a recipe dating back to 1835. Ivor's first shop was founded in King Street in Plymouth in 1934 and moved to Cornwall Street after the Blitz. In addition to large (dinnerplate-sized) pasties, Dewdney's also offer 'field gun' proportioned pasties: Plymouth is proud of its naval heritage.

The Pembrokeshire Pasty, made with lamb and mint, has started production in North Wales. It came about after Cornish baker Elaine Ead, who teaches pasty-making at her shop in Padstow, travelled to Wales to show enthusiasts how to craft a

Welsh version. In July 2000 she was also part of a Government-backed mission to encourage the Americans to take up pasty-making, when she attended a trade fair in New York. The former Celtic, Middlesborough and Republic of Ireland international footballer Chris Morris sells Cornish pasties at his shop in Hartlepool. Chris, who was born in Newquay, puts the secret of his success down to the pastry. His parents were high-class butchers in Cornwall and he says they inherited a recipe 'to die for' from a little old lady who used to bring pasties into their shop every Friday for them to sell.

Sometimes the calibre of pasties found outside the Duchy under the banner of 'Cornish' has caused uproar. In 1993, members of the Chester and Wrexham Cornish Society became so fed up with the number of specimens being passed off as Cornish pasties, they decided to do something about it. They asked the Cornish branch of the National Association of Master Bakers about setting up a competition. The Master Bakers liked the idea of establishing a standard of pasty excellence and they launched an annual competition, with prizes of silver cups and certificates of commendation. The first event was held at the Royal Cornwall Show in Wadebridge in June 1993. I am indebted to Phil Hosken, editor of *Cornish World*, for passing on some of the judges' findings:

In several cases, the location of the contents and the shape of the pasty before crimping, resulted in the crimper having a large piece of pastry left over at the end of the crimp. The pastry would then been crimped into a tail and turned back on the pasty where it was clearly stuck in place with a heavy thumbprint. There may have been some good reason for having such a great wodge of disposable pastry at one end of the pasty a hundred or so years ago to guard the eater against the possible ingestion of arsenic transferred from his hands. This is 1993 and the judges felt it was high time that the indigestible lump was carefully cut off as the crimping progressed to leave a pleasing, edible and acceptable shape. The clear thumb-prints were also off-putting...

One or two pasties had so much onion that they were pungent. We believed that they were so 'strong' that customers could well have complained...

The size of the gap hole in the top in some cases was large enough for a well-fed bluebottle to enter and leave. Whilst we had no evidence that this ever happened, the existence of such a large, dark orifice tended to turn stomachs over and so set the judges against them.

Another reason for creating a Cornish-based pasty competition arose from the furore that erupted at a pie and pasty competition the year before. This event was organised by the National Association of Master Bakers in Birmingham. The winner of the competition was a baker from Huddersfield who submitted an un-crimped pasty made of lamb, peas, sweetcorn and potato. Second place went to a piece of puff pastry with minced vegetable and meat like a patty, folded over like a turnover. Six years later, insult was added to injury when the same Huddersfield baker scooped the championship for a second time, again with his 'unconventional' pasty. The Huddersfield pasty caused a big stir - numerous press reports, radio and TV broadcasts spotlighted the pasty that 'broke all the rules'. Nothing inflames Cornish people more than 'outsiders', particularly culinary experts, daring to lay down the law about the county's favourite dish. People outside the Duchy just don't seem to realise what a sensitive subject the pasty is - even when they may have Celtic roots. Celebrity chef Antony Worrall Thompson cooked up a storm early in 2001 when he dubbed the Cornish pasty 'bland' on his BBC television show *Food and Drink*. Mr Worrall Thompson, whose great-great-great-great-great-great grandfather was Mayor of Truro in 1797, featured the pasty after it was voted Britain's 12th most popular dish in a newspaper poll. He suggested it should be spiced up with pre-cooked beef and vegetables, Worcestershire sauce, thyme and cayenne pepper. Living even more dangerously, he then crimped the pasty with a fork. The TV chef later ate humble pie for the upset he caused in Cornwall: 'I admit I was a little indiscreet by adding an ingredient from another county,' he said. 'Apologies Cornwall - but surely all dishes must evolve. Where would Henry Ford have been if he hadn't improved on his first car?'

In 1999, William Grimes, a top American food critic, bit off more than he could chew when he condemned the Cornish pasty in an article in *The New York Times*. Other journalists sank their teeth into Mr Grimes when he claimed the pasty was 'only good for being used as a doorstop'. The fallout included the ceremonial burning of a Stars and Stripes flag outside the Lizard Pasty Shop. The owner, award-winning pasty maker Ann Muller, later apologised for her actions. Reflecting on the furore, Mr Grimes said: 'The flag, which was nylon, melted a little but but did not actually catch fire. Here was the problem in a nutshell: too many of Cornwall's pasty makers seem to go for the cheapest ingredients.'

Although surprised by the strength of the reaction to his comments the American critic was unrepentant. 'It's possible that I didn't hit the right shop but when you strike out twenty-four or so times in a row you get to wonder', he said. 'What I found was really awful - meat apportioned stingily; a maximum of about a tablespoon; a potato-to-meat ratio of about ten to one. The only really palate appeal is if they put a bit of pepper on it.' Mr Grimes went on to call for better quality pasties in Cornwall: 'If it is something they're proud of, it's a regional resource - they should protect it and present it in its best light and they should be the first to rally behind me and demand a better pasty.'

His words have turned out to be prophetic. The industry is now trying to improve the image of the county's most famous food. A major campaign was launched in June 2000 to protect the Cornish pasty under European law. If the bid is successful, EU rules will stop producers outside the Duchy from calling their pasties 'Cornish'. There is an encouraging precedent. In 1998 the European Commission decided that clotted cream could only be described as Cornish if it was made in the county. Similar commercial protection applies to Italian Olive Oil, Jersey Royal potatoes, Roquefort cheese and Newcastle Brown Ale.

Pasty manufacturers throughout Cornwall have backed the campaign. They welcome any effort to distinguish the Cornish pasty from some of the more dubious snacks made outside the county that trade on its good name. But a long, drawn-out process must be followed before Brussels will even contemplate a request to ringfence the pasty. The Ministry of Agriculture, Fisheries and Food (MAFF) has advised that an application for European Protected Geographical Indication (PGI) status will only be successful if the pasty's cultural (and economic) significance to Cornwall can be proved. MAFF says that establishing the pasty's heritage is particularly important, as there is no agreement on the definitive recipe or shape of a Cornish pasty and many raw ingredients come from outside the county.

Cornwall County Council has appealed for people to submit documents, photographs and family stories about the pasty's past to support the PGI application. In October 2000 a special 'pasty summit' was held in Truro - a conference to further the cause of this initiative. Delegates included experts from MAFF, Women's Institute members, pasty makers and wheat, potato and beef producers. Local MPs and some European Members of Parliament have also pledged their support for the Pasty Campaign.

The road to pasty protection will doubtless be a long and hard one - but if the campaign succeeds, the long-term rewards for the Cornish economy should be great.

Pasty phenomena

HAVING perfected a portable, self-contained convenience food in the 19th century, in recent times the Cornish have gone out of their way to create totally impractical giant pasties. These monstrous creations have more in common with the spectacular oversized pies made for medieval banquets. They test their bakers' skills to the limit and are triumphantly paraded on great public occasions.

A 2ft long pasty was made for a Cornish soldier serving at the front in the First World War. It would have been a poignant reminder of life back home but it is unclear whether it ever got there.

In July 1985, at the rally of Cornwall's Young Farmers' Clubs, a new world record was claimed for the largest-ever pasty. Measuring 32ft 1ins, it comprised 40lb of pastry, 20lb of potatoes and 15lb each of beef, onions and turnips. The giant pasty took four hours to make and three hours to crimp and was baked in four eight-foot sections in a specially built oven.

More recently a pasty was made to resemble a large green Wellington boot. It was raffled for Green Wellie Day - a fundraising campaign for South West farmers whose cattle and sheep were being devastated by Foot and Mouth disease. The pasty, baked by The Homemade Cake Shop in Tavistock, measured 18 by 10 inches, and despite its garish green colour (edible vegetable dye) was eagerly devoured.

A giant replica of a pasty is paraded at the home and away games of Cornwall's rugby team and is symbolically hoisted over the posts at important matches. The custom began in 1908 when Lakes Pottery in Truro made three ceramic pasties as mascots for the first ever appearance of a Cornish side in a rugby championship final. The game was played at Redruth. One pasty was hung on the goalposts but during the first three minutes it fell down and smashed. Despite this, Cornwall beat Durham 17-3. One pasty was presented to the losing team and the other passed in perpetuity to the Cornwall Rugby Association.

Perhaps the most unusual oversized pasty is the one that is paraded with much (mock) pomp and ceremony through the streets of Fowey every year. Its dimensions are hardly record-breaking - 6ft by 18 inches - but it is what the port's good citizens do with their pastry plaything that is so entertaining.

Nobody knows quite how and why the custom started, but a giant pasty was first made at a bakery in Fowey in the early 1960s. When that closed in the mid-Seventies, production switched to Polruan Bakery just across the river, where the oven was big enough to uphold the tradition. It has continued at Polruan ever since and each year, during Regatta Week, the Giant Pasty Ceremony draws thousands of spectators.

Preparing and baking the pasty takes several days and requires 15lb of pastry, 20lb of chopped steak, fifteen onions, 15lb turnip, thirty-five potatoes and 14oz of seasoning. When cooked, the pasty weighs around 120lbs. It has to be carried on a stretcher by four men. Ignoring the ancient superstition about pasties and boats, they convey their cornucopian cargo across the river to Fowey on a pontoon towed by a motor vessel. Throughout its journey, the pasty is accompanied by thirty or so members of

Hanging the ceramic pasty on the crossbar at the County Championship final, Cornwall against Durham at Redruth in 1908.

Fowey Town Band who have spent at least two hours 'warming up' in a local hostelry. Dressed in colourful costumes (a different theme each year), the bandsmen produce what can be best described as a cacophony from oil drums, bugles and whistles. They are under strict instructions not to play anything musical; indeed, anyone caught producing a recognisable tune has to buy a round of drinks for the rest of the band.

When the entourage eventually reaches the steps to the King of Prussia Inn, the giant pasty is ceremonially cut, usually by one of the pilots from the Red Arrows aerobatic team who perform an annual fly-past during Fowey Regatta week. The contents are then sliced up and quickly devoured by hundreds of waiting children. Occasionally, the Fowey Town Band produces an elaborate replica of the giant pasty deliberately to mislead spectators. The 'great pretender' has included one filled with pigeons; another that exploded in front of the crowds and another that suddenly released a skeleton. During the recession-hit late 1980s, the replica became a tiny pasty. One year, the crowds were treated to a prank that stretched the imagination and ingenuity of its perpetrators to the limit. As the giant pasty was being carefully ferried across the river, it slipped off its stretcher and tumbled overboard. The spectators' anxious expressions turned rapidly to wide grins when a 'shark' (a remotely controlled fin) appeared on the scene and chased round frantically in search of the capsized cargo.

From giant pasties - to the more diminutive ones favoured by striptease artists in America. 'Pasties' in this case have nothing to with providing sustenance for performers in between exotic routines. The term describes a sort of flimsy bra that covers stripteasers' nipples and comes from the slang for fake or 'paste' jewellery. The first recorded usage of the word in this sense was in May 1961, when *The Washington Post* reported that 'Miss Mason was lying on the floor with nothing on except the scantiest of brassieres, known in the trade as 'pasties'.' Three years later, *Punch* informed its readers that 'the young ladies of the Folies Bergere in New York have been bidden to wear, in the cause of innocence, two 'pasties'.' Go-go dancers in New York in the Seventies were not allowed to perform completely nude; they wore G-strings and nipple-covering pasties. For the dancers to get a tip, the pasties usually had to come off. Australians have also clasped the more risque meaning of pasties to their linguistic bosom. *The Sunday Truth* in Brisbane revealed in November 1969 that 'stripper Sharon was promoting a Valley nightclub, wearing nothing on top but a couple of pasties to keep her modest.' It is unclear whether Sharon and others of her profession favoured side or top-crimped pasties, but doubtless their audiences came back for second helpings...

Whilst strippers might have protected their modesty with strategically placed pasties, in July 1999 two women in East London defended themselves against a robber with a strategically aimed pasty. An intruder armed with a knife struck at a bakery in Whitechapel Road as staff were counting the day's takings. As Alan Parsons fled for the door with a handful of cash, the ladies behind the counter hit back. 'Sureshot' Tricia Beaton grabbed a Cornish pasty, aimed, and hit Parsons square between the shoulders. Baking trays were also hurled. Mrs Beaton and her colleague Edith Loughlin then tackled the robber outside the shop, marched him back inside and recovered the stolen cash. A judge at the Old Bailey awarded the women £100 each for their bravery and sentenced Parson to three and a half years in jail. Afterwards Mrs Beaton said: 'There was just the one pasty, to be honest - but it was a direct hit and it certainly slowed him down. I'm a pretty good shot.' Mrs Loughlin added: 'He called me a rude name and that made us very angry.'

The incident in East London wasn't the first time a pasty had proved effective as a weapon. One was put to rather gruesome use in 1853, when a Mrs Pellow from Calstock in East Cornwall murdered her child with arsenic and tried to poison her husband in a similar way. *The Royal Cornwall Gazette* reported:

A verdict of wilful murder was returned against the child's mother, and also against a man named Tregay, whom it appears procured the arsenic for her, and with whom she eloped after the child's death. It appears that she attempted to kill her husband a little while before, by putting poison in a pasty which she prepared for him, and which he took with him to the mine where he went to work, but after eating some of it he became sick, and after drinking some warm salt and water, vomited it up again. A dog having eaten the remainder, died almost immediately.

It wouldn't have been too hard for Pellow and Tregay to obtain their deadly ingredients. Calstock was an important area for arsenic mining in the 19th century. The couple, who were apprehended in bed together at St Austell, were probably hanged for their actions.

A sporting postcard congratulating the South African rugby team for their win against Cornwall at Redruth in 1906.

Pasty Pilgrims

Wherever in the world a hole is sunk in the ground, you will be sure to find a Cousin Jack at the bottom of it, searching for metal. (Anon)

IN the second half of the 19th century, the plummeting price of tin drove tens of thousands of Cornish miners (Cousin Jacks) to find work abroad in the silver and gold mines of America, the great copper mines of South Australia and the diamond mines of South Africa. And wherever the Cousin Jacks went, so did their wives (Cousin Jennies), and so too did the Cornish pasty. Like Cornish wrestling and Methodism, the pasty became a way of life - an expression and celebration of the international Cornish identity in mining boom towns all over the world. The legacy of those Cornish pilgrims can be seen in those same towns today. Descendants of those 19th century pioneers still make pasties with recipes handed down through generations.

Cornish mining 'know-how' was in much demand overseas but the great exodus of the Duchy's miners and their families was propelled by harsh economic necessity. Cornish copper production hit a new high in the 1850s but the mines were getting deeper and more expensive to work. Competition was emerging in America, Chile, Cuba and South Australia where costs of production and marketing were much lower. The effects were devastating. Cornish copper crashed, tin production suffered the same fate and many mines spiralled into terminal decline. By 1896 the Cornish industry was facing extinction, with only nine mines still in production. With little opportunity of other employment in Cornwall, many miners packed their bags and headed overseas.

It is estimated that between 1860 and 1900 Cornwall lost more than 100,000 people - a third of its population. Cornish miners had already been working in Mexico in the 1820s and in the lead deposits of Wisconsin in the 1830s. In the 1840s Cornish emigrants filed over to the iron mines on the shores of Lake Huron in Canada. Hundreds of Cornish miners clamoured to become 'Forty-niners' when gold was discovered in California. Grass Valley and Nevada City became mainly Cornish towns and the Cousin Jacks blazed a trail across America. They toiled and settled in Michigan, North Carolina, Utah, New Mexico, Arizona and Colorado. Many of the mines are closed today, their riches exploited long ago, but the Cornish settlers have left their mark. Cornish cooking - particularly pasty-making - is still highly regarded and frequently practised.

During the making of our BBC television documentary *Pasties Away!* in 1996, we travelled to the former gold mining site of Eureka about fifty miles outside Salt Lake City. Cornish miners worked and settled in Eureka in the late 19th century and the town's small museum contains many photographs and artefacts testifying to the influence of the Cousin Jacks and Jennies. Eureka is something of a ghost town today but a small population of mostly elderly citizens has remained, despite the bitter cold and heavy snowfalls in Utah's mountains. There's a strong sense of community in Eureka and many townsfolk proudly claim to be descendants of Cornish emigrants. The Cornish influence struck home to us during our short but memorable visit when we were invited to one of Eureka's regular pasty get-togethers in a community hall. Tables were laid out, mugs of steaming, sweet tea prepared and pasties, baked to traditional Cornish recipes, were handed out and enjoyed by all.

One ingredient in Eureka's pasties that seemed to be a departure from its ethnic roots was a product called 'rutabaga'. It transpired that rutabaga is the term widely used in America for swede. Rutabaga is likely to be Swedish in origin, as seeds from the plant grown in Sweden were sent to Scotland in 1786 and reached Cornwall a few years later. The longer rooted turnip that was common in the farm worker's pasty until the end of the 18th century gave way to the shorter Swedish turnip (swede) in the next century. Unlike the rest of Britain, the Cornish have adopted the vegetable but not its name and confusingly still refer to it as 'turnip'.

Cornish settlements were established in Wisconsin in the early 1800s as a result of migration to the lead mines. Long after the heyday of these mines, pockets of Cornish culture and tradition can still be found today. It is fascinating to see how many customs have survived and how they have been absorbed and adapted in their new cultural settings. For example, early Cornish settlers in Linden, Wisconsin called their pasties 'Teddy Wedgers'. Teddy is a corruption of 'tattie' (potatoes), while wedgers derived from the pasty's shape. A pasty shop in nearby Madison still uses the name Teddy Wedgers today. Jim Jewell, in his book *Cornish in America* (1990), says other Cornish foods have become part of Linden life. These include saffron cake or buns, tea biscuits, seedy biscuits, scalded cream and a cup of 'tay'. The pasty though, reigns supreme:

Come into Linden when the local American Legion Auxiliary is having one of its pasty sales and stop near the Post Office. Immediately you will begin to smell that wonderful unique aroma of pasties being baked in the nearby Community Hall and Legion Hall ovens. The smell permeates the Post Office, where even the stamps are likely to taste like pasty, if your imagination so allows.

The Linden pasty is made along traditional lines; layers of cut beef, potatoes and onions with a crimped pastry case. Acceptable alternatives are the pork and egg pasty, or the Herby Pie consisting of a 'generous fistful of green onion tops, a handful of lettuce leaves and cubed ham or pork, along with egg and seasoning'.

The late Dr A.L. Rowse, a great authority on Cornish history, visited the town of Butte in Montana in 1969. His book *The Cornish in America* explores the influence of the Cornish emigrants who worked in Butte's copper mines in the late 1870s. On the subject of the pasty, however, Dr Rowse takes issue with the authors of another book called *Copper Camp*:

The authors of *Copper Camp* seem to think that it is a Butte speciality: 'The Camp at once adopted the pasty as its own. Today it is as much a part of Butte as the ore dumps. There are few other cities where it may be found. Possibly among the copper mines of Michigan or the Coeur d'Alenes [Idaho]. Elsewhere it is alien.' On the contrary:

wherever two or three Cornishmen are gathered together, there is the pasty; it is fast becoming ubiquitous. Moreover, I should point out a variation: in the American form of pasty the meat is diced; at home in Cornwall, never: it is always sliced.

Copper Camp was at least right about Michigan. It has a great pasty pedigree. The Cornish moved to Michigan's Upper Peninsula in the 1850s when the first copper and iron mines opened. Miners kept their pasties at least body-warm in a chest pocket, or reheated them underground on a mining shovel held over headlamp candles. In the 1950s tourists would seek out the best pasties at stands along highways, or in the restaurants of small towns like Houghton, Hancock, Calumet and South Range. Cooks vied to produce the best pasty, and, taking a leaf from their Cornish ancestors, recipes would be endlessly discussed and secrets closely guarded. Community groups had pasty sales to raise funds. Despite heavy competition from fast food outlets, the pasty is still proving commercially successful in Michigan today. Many towns in the state, with populations of about 20,000, support six to ten pasty shops. At least one enterprising firm has started a pasty franchising operation. Franchisees can set up their own 'pasty parlours' in purpose-built stores or shopping malls. There's even a 'drive-thru' option.

America also has several websites devoted solely to the pasty. One commercial venture boasts 'Past-E-mail', a 'Pasty Weather Desk', and a 'Pasty Cam' showing televised pictures of pasties in production. An internet search brings up numerous pasty recipes, including this one offering advice on eating a pasty:

The recipe is from the Lowery family of Nagaunee and was given to my mother by Madelyn's son, Bud. Bud is the Principle [sic] of the Junior High School where my mom taught Home Ec and gave her the recipe with the following instructions: To eat the Pasty, cut it in half, pick it up, douse with Ketchup and start biting. Wash it down with Orange Soda.

Even the acerbic *New York Times* critic William Grimes might balk at the thought of dousing a pasty with tomato sauce. Whilst denouncing the average Cornish-made pasty as 'hopelessly bland', he does at least have a few words of praise for New York's only pasty-maker, Myers of Keswick: 'The pasty sold at Myers is an elongated rectangle rather than a half-moon shape, the beef is ground rather than diced and the boiled potato is a paste rather than slices, but the pie is quite good and very traditional in spirit.' The Myers pasty, he adds, has a proper Cornish crimp running along the top but 'unlike most Cornish pasties, the Myers pasty is about two-thirds meat.'

American newspapers occasionally run guides to 'British-style' pubs for their ex-pat readers and Anglophiles. Among the establishments included in a *Los Angeles Times* survey in December 1998, there was Ye Olde King's Head in Santa Monica. 'It makes a good, faintly spicy Scotch egg and a ghastly Welsh rarebit,' while its Cornish pasty 'has a plain hamburger filling'. The Crown and Anchor Sports Pub and Grub in Thousand Oaks serves a Cornish pasty 'filled with beef, peas and carrots'.

Australia has been just as significant as America in the story of the globetrotting Cornish. The very first mineral finds in

Australia were made at Glen Osmond near Adelaide in 1841 by two Cornish miners. The discovery of copper brought Cornish miners flocking to Kapunda and Burra in the mid-1840s. Three of the Burra townships were given Cornish names - Redruth, Lostwithiel and Copperhouse - and miners supped at The Cornish Arms, The Ancient Briton and The Redruth Arms. Cornish wrestling was a popular pastime, the Duke of Cornwall's birthday was observed and, of course, the pasty became part of the Cornish-Australian way of life. (As it did in New Zealand, another important destination for Cornish migrants). In the 1850s the Victorian Gold Rush brought thousands of Cornish miners to Bendigo. In her book *Where Now Cousin Jack?* (1998), Ruth Hopkins describes the Cornish Methodist influences in Bendigo, the building and burning of bonfires (a Cornish mid-summer night tradition), and the singing of Cornish carols. She also studies the pasty's ancestry:

One could not even hazard a guess at how many Cornish pasties have been baked and eaten in the Bendigo district. Which product has little or no resemblance to the product baked and sold under this name in Melbourne today. Nevertheless, there are those in the district nurtured on pasties as a regular part of their diet who are neither aware of their origin or why they were a regular comestible, particularly in this and other mining districts. Their importance in Bendigo is recognised in this rhyme:

Crusty, juicy succulent,
Cornish pasties ever meant

The heartening of gallant men -
Cornwall's famed Tre Pol and Pen,
Toothsome provender I ween,
Titillating nostrils keen
Piping hot and good to see
How your savour calls to me.

Many Cornish pasty baking contests were held at local bazaars and fairs. In 1914, Fire Brigade demonstrations were held in Bendigo, after which members of the Fire Brigades Board were entertained with a Cornish pasty supper. Bendigo's offerings were pronounced 'typically Cornish in every respect.'

The copper triangle of Kadina, Moonta and Wallaroo is known as Australia's Little Cornwall. The area celebrates its Cornish roots with a bi-annual festival called 'Kernewek Lowender', which means 'Cornish happiness'. The event draws thousands of visitors, many of them in Victorian costume. At the first festival in 1997, 8,000 Cornish pasties were consumed. Demand was so strong, the local bakery had to sweep the mill's floor to get enough flour for the pasties!

Towards the end of the 19th century, the discovery of gold and diamonds lured thousands of Cornish miners to South Africa. Johannesburg had its own Cousin Jacks' Corner, where ex-pats would meet to exchange news from home or discuss job prospects. The Ferreira Deep Mine was said to be manned almost entirely by former Dolcoath miners. Graham B. Dickason, author of *Cornish Immigrants to South Africa* (1978), says South Africa's culinary heritage comes from so many sources it is difficult to pin-point origins. But he adds 'the Cornish Pasty need have no worry about its source'. Pasties were made solid enough to withstand being carried down ladder-roads in miners' 'mossle-bags'. A church minister was so delighted by the pasty, he wrote this ode:

How dear to my lips is a hot Cornish pasty,
When fondly my missus presents it to view;
It makes my mouth water to see it there steaming,
The meal most delicious that ever I knew.
The twist on its edge and the hole in the middle,
The sight of it gives me an appetite keen.
Some day they may find out a meal that is better,
But up to this time it has never been seen.
   A good Cornish pasty, a hot Cornish pasty,
   A big Cornish pasty, its praises I'll tell.
Just take what you will it is good in a pasty;
Potatoes and turnips and onions will do:
And carrots and parsnips, tomatoes and cabbage,
Leeks, beans and beats, and broccoli too.

Then put in the beef, the pork or the mutton,
Some liver or kidney, some chicken or veal;
Or maybe some rabbit, or tripe if its tender,
And you will pronounce it a Number One Meal.
   A good turnip pasty, a hot leeky pasty,
   A big chicken pasty, you'll like it so well.
And when it is Lent, put some fish in your pasty,

A pilchard or mackerel, a herring or hake;
A trout or a codfish, some sardines or salmon,
And you will be surprised at what a meal it will make.
Or if you like fruit you can easily use it,
Just put some black currants inside of your pasty,
Some gooseberries, raspberries, plums or some apples,
Or maybe some rhubarb will just suit your taste.
    A good mackerel pasty, a strawberry pasty,
    A great big jam pasty, O, isn't that swell?
You may eat it at home or when on a journey;
You can carry it with you in mine or store.
Never mind plates or dishes, a paper bag holds it.
When you've eaten one pasty, you're anxious for more.
The Germans were fighting on sauerkraut and sausage,
They thought they would win but now they are wiser;
A lot of our soldiers were feeding on pasties,
And when they got busy, good-bye to the Kaiser.
    So here's to the pasty, the good Cornish pasty.
    We'll never get tired its praises to tell.

The Cornish also emigrated to Mexico during the late 19th and early 20th centuries. In Hidalgo State, Cousin Jacks settled to work in the region's mines. Among their legacies they left soccer - Mexico's most popular sport - and 'pastes', a local adaptation of Cornish pasties. In the capital Pachuca, the pastes now include various hot spicy flavours like chile and mole.

In more recent times, the pasty has picked up a small following in Mashiko in Japan. This has nothing at all to do with Cornish miners. It is entirely due to the collaboration of two internationally renowned potters, Bernard Leach from St Ives and Shoji Hamada from Japan. Leach worked alongside Hamada in Japan in the 1920s; together they also set up the Leach Pottery studio in St Ives. While in Cornwall, Hamada obviously developed a taste for pasties and by the time he returned to Japan in 1924, his craft skills had extended to Cornish cooking. Nowadays Shoji Hamada's descendants in Mashiko still perform the ancient ceremony of pasty-making. This was demonstrated when Bernard Leach's grandson Philip visited Mashiko during a lecture tour in October 1996. Philip was introduced to Shoji's son Shinsaku, and after seeing a remarkable collection of his grandfather's old pots for the first time, Philip was then entertained with a meal of Cornish pasties.

Pasty Past

THE pasty consumed by millions of people today as a savoury takeaway meal has a pedigree dating back to the Middle Ages. Despite strong links with Cornwall, the county was not its birthplace. In fact, it was at least 500 years B.C. (Before Cornwall) when the pasty first appeared. Far from being the humble fare of the common man, it started life as an exotic food enjoyed almost exclusively by royalty and the upper classes.

Meat - particularly venison, beef, lamb or mutton - was eaten in enormous and extravagant quantities at medieval banquets and feasts. Huge portions of meat were dressed with rich gravies, seasoned, spiced and sweetened with dried fruits. As well as roast dishes, pies or pasties filled with meat and fine sauces were also popular. The wealthy ate some vegetables, but hated them - vegetables were the staple diet of the poor. But they couldn't eat meat all the time - England was then largely a Catholic country. Wednesdays, Fridays and Saturdays were meatless days and throughout Lent, eggs and other dairy foods were also forbidden. So salmon, trout, and even porpoise pasties made their way to the high tables. At Lent you could eat 'porpoise baked with spices in pastry, made in the manner of pasty'.

The idea of tucking into a close relative of the dolphin might seem repugnant to us now, but in the Middle Ages it was quite common. There are several porpoise recipes in *The Forme of Cury* - a roll of ancient English cookery, compiled in 1390 by the master cooks of King Richard II. They include 'furmente with porpays' (porpoise stew), 'porpays in broth' and 'puddyng porpays'.

One of the oldest references to the pasty crops up in the 13th century. Henry III (1216-1272) was particularly fond of lampreys, a fish which resembles an eel and has no scales. The lamprey has a mouth like a sucker, pouch-like gills, seven spiracles or apertures on each side of the head and a fistula or opening on the top of the head. Lots of these evil-looking creatures were consumed when meat-eating was banned. To ensure a plentiful stock, King Henry had his own weirs on the River Severn and forbade any trade in lampreys during periods of short supply. In 1242 the Bailiffs of Gloucester were 'commanded to send pasties of salmon and lampreys as quickly and frequently as they can to the King.'

We think of today's pasties as half-moon pastry turnovers with either a savoury or sweet filling, while pies are often larger, higher-walled and circular in shape. In medieval times 'pasty' and 'pie' had much the same meaning. Later cookbooks contained recipes for both pasties and pies, side by side but with little differentiation between the two. Early pasties/pies were free-standing pastry containers - the main purpose in medieval cookery: 'Al of pasteiis be walles, Of fleis, of fisse, and rich met' (*Land Cokayne*, written before 1300).

Pastry was made from hot water 'paste' - a robust pastry ideally suited to raised pies. Early recipes speak of 'raising the coffin' - i.e. the pie's sides and bottom. Using a pottery dish is never mentioned. As well as being efficient cooking vessels, pies and pasties were convenient ways of eating meat in gravy before the fork was in general use. A cold pie where the stock was jellied was particularly easy to eat with the fingers. Forks were used for sweetmeats on royal and noble tables in the 14th century but they only emerged as a major item of cutlery during the 17th century. Years later, of course, Cornish farm workers and tin miners revived the hand-held tradition of their medieval ancestors.

Unlike the sturdy and simple Cornish pasty, the medieval pie was a rich, feast day dish filled with mouth-watering titbits. Meat or fish pies also contained delicacies like artichoke bottoms, truffles, kidneys, oysters, mushrooms, raisins, prunes, apples or pears, orange or lemon peel as well as herbs and spices. These exotic dishes were all very well for the high table but the producers of the food, the peasants of the countryside scraped along on a very rudimentary diet. They lived off coarse black bread (barley, rye or bean-flour), milk, cheese, eggs and occasionally bacon or a fowl. Many of the real poor usually ate little more than bread and onions and perhaps a green vegetable like cabbage, washed down with water. Small wonder then, that the pasty should become an object of desire among the lower classes. Geoffrey Chaucer refers to the pasty in *The Canterbury Tales* (1387-1400). In the Prologue to *The Cook's Tale*, he writes:

Now telle on Roger, looke that it be good,
For many a pastee hastow laten bled
(Modern English: 'For many a pasty have you robbed of blood')

Pasty gastronomy also exercised French master chefs in the 14th century. Guillaume Tirel, known as Taillevent, was the chief cook of Charles v and his book *Le Viandier de Taillevent* is one of the most important medieval French recipe collections.

Taillevent had several pasty recipes, including one for 'pastez nourroys' and 'pastez lorez'. Pastez nourroys were Norse pasties comprising finely chopped meat (rabbit), pinenut paste, currants, rich cheese and a little salt. The ingredients were fried and dressed with a rich, spicy sauce. Similarly, pastez lorez were little Lorez pies filled with chopped pork, pinenuts, currants, cheese and salt, then deep fried.

Recipes for 'rich pasties' can be found in *Le Menagier de Paris* - commonly translated as *The Householder of Paris*. It was written in 1395 by an elderly merchant as a book of instruction for his new, 16-year-old wife. The author wanted his young bride to be able to manage their household when he was away, control servants and supervise the cooking of meals. In the section on pastry, a recipe for venison pasty recommends: 'parboiling the venison, skimming and larding it and making pastry: this is the way to make pasties of all fresh venison; and it should be cut in big, long pieces like rolling pins and this is called pasty of larded boiled meat.' For beef pasties: 'Have a good young beef and remove all the fat and the less good parts are cut in pieces to be used for stock and then it is carried to the pastry-cook to be chopped up: and the grease with beef marrow. The meat of a leg of beef is sliced up and put in pastry; and when the pastry is cooked, it is appropriate to throw a wild duck sauce into it.' Mutton pasties should be 'chopped very small with scallions' (shallots or even wild garlic) and for veal pasties 'take the round part of the thigh, put with it almost as much beef fat and with this you make six good pasties in platters.'

A pasty to beat all pasties - for sheer size and variety of

ingredients - is to be found in a 15th century French cookery book, *Du Fait de Cuisine*. Written by Maistre Chiquart Amiczo in 1420, it details a lavish feast prepared for Monseigneur Ayme, the First Duke of Savoy. The guest list included kings, queens, princes, princesses, dukes, duchesses and many members of the nobility. Provisioning the banquet required 100 well-fattened cattle, 130 sheep (also well-fattened), 100 piglets, 200 lambs, 2,000 chickens, 6,000 eggs, thirty loaves of sugar, twenty-five pounds of saffron and forty pounds of pinenuts. Cooking utensils for the feast included twenty large frying pans, a dozen large casks, 100 wooden bowls, twenty iron shovels and twenty rotisseries. And as it was likely the guests would fancy a drink or two, best to order 'two casks of wine - one of white and one of

claret, each of eight sommes [110 gallons], and a good cask of verjous [sugared cider vinegar] of twenty sommes [275 gallons].' Clearly, when it came to 'the making of pastry', M. Chiquart wasn't going to skimp. 'There should be a large and fair building close to the kitchen [...] for two large and fair ovens for making meat and fish pastries, tarts and flans,' he commanded. And the maestro went on to specify exactly how to produce his cocade pasty:

Take beef and the fair fat from beef kidneys and let this be chopped very small, and let him take care that when the beef is dismembered he has all of the marrow, and then put it in his pasty; and then let him take his spices well and properly, that is ginger, grains of paradise, saffron and salt, and all these things in measure. And the pastry-cook will be well advised to make the crust of the pastry so large, well and honestly in several compartments so large that in each can be put that which one devises for it: in the best should be lodged the beef pasty. In another compartment should be put a lamprey, in another compartment should be put a salmon, and in another should be put a pigeon, in another small birds which should be stuffed with guein cheese and beef marrow, another compartment large pieces of fresh trout, and in the last compartment - if you do not want any more things - capons.

The feasting tradition continued in England in the 15th century and well into the 16th century. Menus for royal banquets were still composed almost entirely of meat and fish while raw vegetables and fruit were regarded with great suspicion by Tudor diners. With the dissolution of the monasteries in the 1530s, vast areas of countryside passed into lay hands. The landed gentry emerged as a new prosperous and influential class. Their increasing affluence enabled them to spend more on travel, recreation and luxury goods. Keen to imitate the culinary standards of the royal household, ladies eagerly devoured the growing number of cookery books. For instance, Gervase Markham's *The English Housewife* (1649) contains a menu for what he calls 'a more humble feast':

Sixteen is a good proportion for one course... I'll make the list complete but brief: beef with mustard; boiled capon; boiled beef; roast chine of beef; roast neat's [calf's] tongue; roast pig; baked chewets [small, round, fried pasties]; roast goose; roast swan; roast turkey; roast haunch of venison; venison pasty; kid with a pudding in the belly; olive pie; several capons; a custard or doucets [sweet apples].

The 16th and 17th centuries saw a huge rise in the popularity of venison pasties. Once the sole preserve of kings and nobles, deer hunting remained an aristocratic privilege but venison became more widely available in country parks and farms. To combat toughness, meat was hung to mature it and break down the fibres, or heavily spiced or pickled to tenderise it. Deer meat was well suited to the pasty; it took a lot of slow cooking and without protection would have been very hard. So enclosing it in pastry would have been like wrapping a joint in foil nowadays to contain the moisture. Literature of the Tudor period is peppered with references to venison pasties. In Act I of Shakespeare's *The Merry Wives of Windsor* (1597), Page welcomes Falstaff, Bardolph, Slender, Simple, Nym and Pistol by saying: 'Come, we have a hot venison pasty to dinner: come gentlemen, I hope we shall drink down all unkindness.' The diaries of Samuel Pepys (1660-1669) contain many references to venison pasty. To Pepys, good food was one of the great pleasures of life, and in his lifetime he would have witnessed great changes. Vegetables, fruits and salads became more popular; tea, coffee, chocolate and even ice cream made their first appearance and knives, forks and spoons were widely manufactured. The pasty was probably still hand-held but it was no longer the crude, hot-water crust container of medieval times. Cold fat was being used to make a shorter and crisper pastry, both shortcrust and puff. In Pepys' diary we accompany the young civil servant into his world of food - in London taverns as well as his own dining room. Often he writes of 'dining on a good venison pasty and being mighty merry' but on a few occasions, the experience was less than savoury:

August 1ˢᵗ 1667. Dined at Sir William Pen's, only with Mrs Turner and her husband, on a venison pasty, that stunk like a devil. However, I did not know it until dinner was done. We had nothing but only this, and a leg of mutton, and a pullet or two.

Pepys might well have described Sir William's cook as a 'wag-pasty' - a 17th century term for a mischievous rogue - because this meal sounds almost like a practical joke. That phrase - 'I did not know it until dinner was done' - suggests that Pepys was later troubled by the onset of wind. Perhaps he was unaware of the danger posed by his diabolical dish because the flavour was disguised by one of the sweet, spicy or fruity sauces that often accompanied cooked meat.

The distinction between a sweet and savoury dish was much less clear and important to our ancestors than it is to us. Savoury dishes could contain raisins or apples, sweet pies could include meat. In 1719 a French visitor to England, one Monsieur Misson, admired a Christmas pasty, observing: 'It is a great Nostrum, the composition of this Pasty: it is a most learned Mixture of Neats-tongues, Chicken, Eggs, Sugar, Raisins, Lemon and Orange Peel, various Kinds of Spicery, etc.' Dishes were sweetened, more than they were seasoned with salt and pepper, until the mid-18th century. There is a sign of the changing times in a rare copy of *The London Cook - or the Whole Art of Cookery Made Easy and Familiar* (1762), which used to belong to the Polwhele family, 18th century Cornish landowners. The volume is held in the Cornwall Record Office in Truro. Its recipe for venison pasty (reproduced on page 86 of this book) clearly demonstrates the move away from sugar and spice towards salt and black pepper. Combined sweet and savoury pasties later went underground with Cornish miners, but even these treats were divided into separate 'main course' and 'pudding' compartments.

By the second half of the 18th eighteenth century the potato was becoming increasingly popular, nearly 200 years after Sir Walter Ralegh and the great Cornish adventurer Sir Richard Grenville first brought it back from Virginia. As a complement

A working lunch c 1905.

to meat, the potato served as an appealing alternative to pastry and so, by the 19th century, the ancient British tradition of the pie was in decline. The point of the pie had always been that it was a complete, self-contained dish which didn't need accompaniments. The increasing use of cutlery also contributed to the decline of savoury pies and pasties.

However, by a strange twist of fate, the potato was to play a vital role in the pasty's revival. Miners and labourers required plenty of carbohydrates to sustain them for long working hours, as well as meat to maintain their energy levels and vitamin-rich vegetables to boost their vision in poorly lit areas. They also needed a self-contained meal but not one to be eaten with knives and forks in a dining room. Cornwall was made for the pasty - and the pasty was remade by labourers and miners in Cornwall.

Pasty parallels

THE emigration of Cornish miners to far-flung lands has brought about numerous pasty imitations and spin-offs. For centuries other countries have also produced their own home-grown meat or fish pastry-wrapped parcels.

The Italians make panzerotti - a turnover of pork, egg and strong cheeses with a stuffing made of olives, onions, capers, anchovies and tomatoes. The ingredients are wrapped in pizza dough and fried in hot oil. In the Pugliese capital of Bari, panzerotti are traditionally made for the feast of St Anthony Abbot in January. In Finland, North Karelia is the birthplace of Karelian pasties. Although eaten throughout Finland, the Koensuu version, spread with real butter, is apparently the genuine article. Its thin rye crust is filled with rice and shaped like a moccasin. Fish pasties came to Finland from the east. Vendace, perch or rainbow trout and pork are wrapped in a rye pastry case and baked slowly at low heat. In Serbia, 'pastetice od sira-skute' are Yugoslavian pastry turnovers, filled with ham. The pastry is made from flour, butter and cottage cheese. In Russia and Poland, left-over meat or fish and vegetables are enclosed in a yeast dough and deep fried.

In Latin America, savoury meat and vegetable-filled empanadas are made with a pastry crust that closely resembles the pasty. 'Empanar' is Spanish for 'to bake in pastry'. Filled with fruit, then can be served as a dessert. Empanadas range in size from the huge empanada gallega - large enough to feed an entire family - to empanaditas - tiny, ravioli sized pastries. Pastelillos are deep-fried Caribbean pasties, containing meat or cheese. They are generally served as an hors d'oeuvre or appetiser.

Closer to home, a Lancashire Foot was a traditional type of pasty often taken down coal pits by miners. Just like feet, they came in pairs, roughly semi-circular in shape so they fitted into an oval carrying tin. A Collier's Foot, also from the north of England, was similar to its Lancashire cousin. Then there is the Priddy Oggie - a West Country pasty filled with bacon, pork and cheese, first made in the late 1960s at The Miner's Arms in Priddy on the Mendip Hills in Somerset.

From Bedfordshire comes the clanger - a rectangular baked pastry with a suet crust, filled with savoury and sweet ingredients at opposite ends. The word 'clanger' is thought to derive from 'clang' - a Northamptonshire dialect word meaning 'to eat voraciously'. Clangers were once a boiled suet roll, similar to plum duff or roly-poly. Like the intermingled sweet and savoury pasties of medieval times, the roll contained a meat filling while the crust was studded with fruit. The Befordshire Clanger, like the Cornish pasty, was a plain substantial food for farm labourers and other manual workers. For the poor, the only meat readily available was bacon. Richer families used good steak or pork.

The Scottish answer to the Cornish pasty is the Forfar Bridie. Typical ingredients include rump or topside steak or venison, Worcestershire sauce (à la Worrall Thompson!), onion, nutmeg, stock and seasoning, all wrapped up in a shortcrust pastry case and baked in a hot oven.

Meanwhile, Cornish pastry dishes are not just confined to the pasty. At the turn of the 20th century, a 'stann'in' pie was made on a baking iron and covered with the baker. When cooked, the top crust was pierced with a small hole through which a quantity of cream (known as 'ream') was poured. Sweet giblet pie was a sort of mince pie containing goose giblets, boiled and chopped fine. Muggety pie was made from selected sheep entrails, flavoured with parsley and enriched with a lot of cream. There was also squab pie, made of fat mutton and apples in alternative layers, plus onions and raisins.

Finally, there is starry-gazey pie - a traditional dish once common in coastal areas of West Cornwall. It is still made each year in the fishing port of Mousehole on December 23, known as Tom Bowcock's Eve. Legend has it that Tom, a local fisherman, saved the community from near-starvation by his daring exploits more than 200 years ago. After weeks of bad weather, when no one could put to sea, he ventured out alone and returned with seven kinds of fish. These were put into a starry-gazey pie - the fish heads poke up through the pastry to 'gaze at the stars'.

Pasty prospects

THE pasty is rich in history and cultural significance and has gone through some remarkable changes in its lifetime. From its early high table beginnings at medieval banquets, to the vegetable-filled black barley crust of 18th century labourers, to the staple diet of miners in Cornwall and across the world, the pasty has proved an enduring and popular portable meal.

Today millions of pasties are made by bakeries offering a wide choice of fillings. Some commercial producers are always on the lookout for new varieties but it is still the traditional, beef, potato, onion and turnip (swede) version that sells the most. As a fast food the pasty has yet to take the world by storm - even though it pre-dates burgers, pizzas and hot-dogs by centuries. Efforts have been made both in the UK and the USA to set up pasty franchise outlets (shops that bake and sell pasties on the premises) but these are still few in number. Perhaps what the pasty needs is a marketing makeover, freshening up its 'crusty' image to appeal to modern cosmopolitan takeaway tastes. On the other hand, it's the pasty's simplicity that arguably provides its greatest appeal. Hot, wholesome and good value, it doesn't require extra sauce or chips. Unlike other takeaway foods that would probably spill if you tried to consume them as you walked around, the pasty with its integral and edible pastry wrapper performs well under the strain of perambulation. And, if you can't manage a whole one, save some for later - just as the miners used to do when they carried them inside their jackets.

In Cornwall, the art of pasty-making is still taken very

seriously. Family recipes are closely-guarded secrets and pasty contests at local shows draw many competitors and spectators. In many households the tradition of baking pasties on certain days of the week is still followed. But the skills that used to be learned at mother's elbow are less a part of domestic life today. Changing work and leisure patterns, different family values, the increased availability of processed and convenience foods, all have taken a toll on the pasty.

Commercial producers in Cornwall are now fighting back. The campaign to protect the Cornish pasty under European law is intended to safeguard the jobs of thousands of workers in a multi-million pound industry. It's a call-to-arms that has united producers, promoters and politicians in defence of the humble oggy. Vital to the campaign's success will be proving the pasty's Cornish heritage and cultural significance. To many the words 'pasty' and 'Cornish' are inseparable. More pasties are made in the Duchy than anywhere else in the UK.

But who's to say that pasties produced east of the Tamar are not just as good - if not better - than some of those made in Cornwall? If the Cornish pasty is ring-fenced then people perhaps baking better versions outside the county would be barred from calling them 'Cornish'. The field would be left clear for Cornish manufacturers of 'hopelessly bland' pasties (as Mr Grimes of *The New York Times* would say) to capitalise heavily on its 'good' name. Unlike Jersey Royal potatoes or Roquefort cheese, Cornish pasty contents can be sourced from anywhere in Britain. It cannot be defined as a truly indigenous food - and historically, Cornwall can only really lay claim to the pasty over the past 200 years.

While the decision-makers in Brussels scratch their heads over these issues, there is another aspect to be considered: if the pasty does earn protected status, will all of its Cornish makers have to produce something of very similar quality and make-up? That would detract from its inherent charm. It is the pasty's diverse flavours and baking methods that make it so appealing.

Whatever decision is made, it won't be an easy one. Cornwall may have lost all its tin mines, but it is fiercely protective of the industry's most famous by-product. The pasty, even in its many forms, is still synonymous with Cornwall. Like the Scottish kilt, or the Welsh dragon, it has become a strong symbol of its region - an edible cultural icon whose pedigree dates back centuries and whose popularity is set for many years to come.

Porthtowan Beach c 1904.

Pasty Patois

Baker-ire or *baker* - cover for flat iron used for baking on peat fires

Bal maidens - women employed in 19th century mines to break up ore

Buccas or *Bockles* - underground Cornish imps (also known as Knackers or Knockers)

Cloam oven - dome-shaped earthenware oven set into an open chimney

Crib - a small meal, or lunch

Crimp - crust of a pasty

Crowst or *crowse* - a luncheon, a feed (Celtic Cornish)

Denner - dinner

Figgy-duff - dough, raisins and fat baked in the form of a pasty (also known as hobbin or hobban)

Flat ire or *flat iron* - iron plate used for baking on peat fires

Fuggan - Cornish heavycake

Grass pasty - made with herbs and pork

Hobbin or *hobban* - dough, raisins and fat baked like a pasty (also called a figgy-duff)

Hoggan - unleavened dough filled with pork (also used to describe a miner's meal bag)

Likky - leek

Mate - meat

Mate an tiddy oggy - meat and potato pasty

Mossle-bag - South African term for miner's meal bag

Neaps - turnips or swede (also known as rutabaga)

Oggy or *oggie* - slang term for pasty

Raw-ream - cream of milk, not scalded

Rutabaga - swede or turnip

Snap - miner's meal

Tetty-hoggan - potato pasty

Tiddie-oggie - a pasty

Turmit or *turmut* - turnip or swede or rutabaga

Teddy Wedger - Wisconsin miners' term for pasty

Windy pasty - pastry case baked empty, then filled with jam

Policemen on their lunch break at the Redruth Exhibition in 1905

Pasty Papers

The Forme of Cury, edited by Samuel Pegge (1780).

Royal Recipes, Michele Brown (Pavilion Books, 1995).

Le Viandier de Taillevent, edited by Terence Scully (Acanthus Books, 1988).

Le Menagier de Paris, Jerome Pichon (1846).

Du Fait de Cusine, Maistre Chiquart, edited by Terence Scully (Vallesia, 1985).

The English Housewife, Gervase Markham (McGill-Queen's University Press, 1986; first printed 1649).

The Cookery of England, Elizabeth Ayrton (Penguin, 1977).

M Misson's Memoirs: Observations in his travels over England, translated from the French by Mr Ozell (1719).

The London Cook, William Gelleroy (1762).

'The Merry Ballad of the Cornish Pasty', Robert Morton Nance (*Cornish Magazine*, Vol. I, 1898).

'Soup on Sundays', *St James Chronicle* (1776).

General View of the Agriculture of the County of Cornwall, G.B. Worgan (1811).

Mines of Devonshire and Cornwall - a report by Dr Charles Burham for The Royal Commission on Children's Employment (1842).

Cornish Homes and Customs, A.K. Hamilton Jenkin (Dent & Sons, 1934).

Fire, Tin and Copper - or Cornwall; its Mines and Miners, Charles Garton Honor (1869).

'The Cornish Cook', H.D. Lowry (*Chambers Journal*, Vol III, March 1900).

Cornwall, Claude Berry (Robert Hale, 1949).

Cornish Recipes, Ancient and Modern, Cornwall Federation of Women's Institutes (1929).

'Recollections of Lanhydrock', Jack Gillespie (*Cornish Life*, October 1985).

Cornish Cookery, Vida Heard (Dyllansow Truran, 1984).

Schoolhouse in the Wind, Anne Treneer (Jonathan Cape, 1946).

England in the 19th Century - Illustrated Itinerary of the County of Cornwall (How & Parsons, 1842).

Cornwall, Dr Philip Payton (Alexander Associates, 1996).

The Cornish in America, A.L. Rowse (Macmillan, 1969).

Cornish in America, Jim Jewell (Cornish Miner Press, 1990).

Where Now Cousin Jack?, Ruth Hopkins (DG Walker, 1998).

Cornish Immigrants to South Africa, Graham B. Dickason (A.A. Balkema, 1978).

Traditional foods of Britain, Laura Mason & Catherine Brown (Prospect Books, 1999).

Pasty Preparation

THESE two recipes come from *The London Cook* by William Gelleroy (1762). The copy owned by the Polwheles - Cornish landowners - is now held in the Cornwall Record Office. See page 73 of this book.

Venison Pasty

'Lay down half a peck of flour, put into it four pounds of butter, beat eight eggs and make the paste with warm water; bone the venison, break the bones, season them with salt and pepper and boil them: with this fill up the pasty when it comes out of the oven: take a pound of beef sewet, cut it into slices, throw pepper and salt upon it: lay the venison in, seasoned pretty high with salt and pepper; set pudding crust round the inside of the pasty, and put in about three-quarters of a pint of water: lay on a layer of fresh butter and cover it. When it comes out of the oven, pour in the liquor you have made of the bones boiled, and shake all well together.'

Beef Pasty

'Take a small rump or sirloin of beef, bone it, beat it very well with a rolling-pin; then, to five pounds of this meat take two ounces of sugar, rub it well in, and let it lie for twenty-four hours; then either wipe it clean, or wash it with a little claret, and season it high with salt, pepper and nutmeg, put it into your paste, and lay over it a pound of butter; close up the pasty, and bake it as much as venison. Put the bones in a pot with just as much water as will cover them, and bake them to make a gravy, and when the pasty is drawn, if it wants liquor, put in some of this gravy.'

THE following recipes come from *Cornish Recipes - Ancient and Modern*, issued by the Cornwall Federation of Women's Institutes in 1929.

Pasty

'Any good pastry may be used but it should not be too flaky nor too rich. A very useful pastry is: 1lb flour, ½ lb lard and suet, ½ teaspoonful salt, mix with water.

When pastry is made, roll out about ¼ inch thick, and cut into rounds with a plate to the size desired.

Lay the rounds on the pastry board with half of the round over the rolling pin and put in the fillings, damp the edges lightly and fold over semi-circle.

Shape the pasty nicely and crimp the extreme edges where it is joined between the finger and the thumb. Cut a slit in the centre of the pasty, lay on a baking sheet and bake in a quick oven, so that it keeps its shape.'

Herby Pasty

'Prepare pastry as for ordinary pasty. Well wash equal quantities of parsley, bits, shallots (early), half quantity spinach, prepare some slices of bacon cut into small pieces and an egg well beaten. Pour boiling water over the parsley, bits and spinach that have been cut into small portions, and let stand for half and hour, well squeeze all moisture out. Put on pastry with the shallots cut finely and the bacon, pinch up the edges of pasty allowing a small portion left open for the egg to be added, finish pinching and bake.'

(This recipe came from the Boscastle branch, who said those mysterious 'bits' were a common herb, believed to be found only along the hedgerows and cliffs of North Cornwall. Gypsies picked it for medicinal purposes).

Starry-Gazey Pasty

'Mawther used to get a herring, clean 'un, and put same stuffin' as what yow do have in mabiers [chicken]; sew 'en up with niddle and cotton, put 'en some daugh made of suet and flour; pinch the daugh up in the middle and lave the heid sticking out one end and tail t'other. They were some nice pasties, too, cooked in a fringle fire with crock and brandis and old furzy tobs.' (Recipe from E.R.)

Stephen Hall's Cornish pasty

THERE are hundreds of recipes for pasties, most of which are variations on the same theme. This recipe makes four medium pasties. It does not pretend to produce the definitive Cornish pasty (the very idea!), but it is nevertheless a good basic recipe. I leave it up to you to decide whether to crimp on the top or the side.

INGREDIENTS:

For the pastry:
450g (1lb) plain flour
113g (4oz) chilled margarine or salted Cornish farmhouse butter
112g (4oz) chilled lard
A little salt

For the filling:
450g (1lb) beef skirt, or chuck steak
2 medium onions
450g (1lb) swede (turnip) or leek (you can combine them)
450g (1lb) potatoes
Knob of Cornish butter
Freshly ground black pepper

For the glaze (optional):
1 egg, beaten

METHOD:

Preheat the oven to 200°C/400°F/Gas Mark 6.

Add a pinch of salt to the flour. Cube the lard, butter or margarine and rub into the flour until it resembles fine breadcrumbs. Add cold water a tablespoonful at a time and mix into a stiff dough. Divide pastry into four, cover and set aside to rest in the refrigerator for at least 20 minutes.

Peel and finely slice the potatoes, onion and swede. Wash, trim and slice leeks if used. Slice beef into small, thin pieces.

Roll out pastry on a floured surface. Place a plate on the pastry and cut round. Pile meat and vegetables in layers in centre of pastry circle and season to taste with salt and pepper. Add a dab of butter on top. Damp the edges of the pastry to help it seal. Fold sides together and crimp. Brush pasty with beaten egg (optional).

Place on a baking tray and cook for about 25 minutes until pastry colours, then reduce heat to 170°C/325°F/Gas Mark 3 for a further 40 minutes. May be eaten hot or cold.

FANCY EXTRAS:

You can add a few drops of beef stock or 50g (2oz) of double cream to each pasty before crimping. The Devonshire pasty was supposed to be made with cream. But bear in mind that a well-cooked pasty will produce its own juice and too much liquid will only leak out.

STEPHEN Hall is a broadcast journalist with more than 25 years' experience in television and radio. He was born in 1952, studied at Hurstpierpoint College in Sussex and gained a Diploma in Communication Studies at Birmingham Polytechnic. Since 1993, he has been a television reporter for BBC South West in Plymouth.

In 1996 he was reporter and co-producer of *Pasties Away!* - a half hour television documentary about the first Cornish pasties to be exported to the USA. The programme was shortlisted for a regional Royal Television Society award.

Stephen won a national British Environmental Media Award in 1999 as the reporter for a BBC South West documentary about the sinking of the container ship *Cita* on the Isles of Scilly.

He is also a part-time lecturer in radio journalism at the College of St Mark and St John in Plymouth. His interests include sailing, pilot gig rowing, sub-aqua diving and cricket. He is writing a book about gig racing for Agre Books.

ACKNOWLEDGEMENTS

I would like to thank the following people who gave me much help and support in writing this book:

Paddy Bradley, Gerald Luke and Clive Benney for their pasty postcards; Viv Hendra for his painting 'The Noonday Rest'; Mark Hannam for his pasty cartoons; Gerard Morgan-Grenville for his drawing of a cloam oven; Jan Gendall for her extensive knowledge of Cornish folklore; Clive Carter for his information about the Cornish Range made at Holman's; Mary Hawke of the Cornwall Federation of Women's Institutes; Phil Hosken, Editor of *Cornish World*; Sally Holden, Curator of the North Cornwall Museum and staff at the Cornwall Record Office, the Cornish Studies Library and the Royal Institute of Cornwall Photographic Collection for the image ref. Mleap.21. My thanks also to Elaine Floyd who taught me how to make a pasty, and to Jonathan and Sara Hudston who encouraged me to pursue this subject.

ABOUT THE PRINTING OF THIS BOOK:
The Cornish Pasty was typeset by Agre Books in Monotype Classic Octavian. The cover was designed by Stuart Brill at Senate Design Ltd in London. The book was printed and bound on 130gsm art paper by R. Booth (Bookbinders) Ltd of Mabe near Penryn in Cornwall. Booth's is a family firm which prints books for several small publishers. Robert and Mary Booth started as a bookbinder's in 1971. In 1977 their son Steven joined the business and the firm expanded into printing.

ABOUT AGRE:

AGRE Books is a small, independent publisher which specialises in non-fiction books about South West subjects. Based in Dorset, it covers the South West peninsula from Bristol and Bath down to the Isles of Scilly.

Agre takes its name from the legend of Actaeon and Diana as told in Ovid's *Metamorphoses*. Ovid names Actaeon's hounds and lists their attributes. 'The thicket-searcher Agre' was the hound with the keenest nose. Agre Books intends to search the thickets of its distinctly rural region to find interesting truths and intriguing stories.

Titles published include:

Islomania (£6.50) by Sara Hudston, with 21 photographs from the Gibson Archive on the Isles of Scilly. Islomania - an obsession with islands. Why are islands so captivating? Using Scilly as its example, this book explores what islands mean to us.

The Wheal of Hope (£9.99). Poems and notes by James Crowden, with 35 black and white pictures by photographer George Wright, whose work has appeared in many national newspapers and magazines. The closure of South Crofty, the last working tin mine in Cornwall, marked the end of 3,000 years of history. This book records what it was like to labour hundreds of fathoms underground and pays tribute to all the men, women and children whose lives shaped Cornwall's unique industrial landscape.

For Love of Williamina (£6.99) by Ralph Rochester, with five illustrations. Williamina Belsches' beauty captured the heart of the young Walter Scott just as he was on the cusp of fame. But she spurned the penniless poet and chose instead to become the dutiful wife of a wealthy baronet. At the age of only 32 she contracted consumption and sought relief in the sea-breezes of Lympstone in Devon, then the haunt of many fashionable invalids. This romantic and moving account tells the story of her final months and gives an unsurpassed picture of East Devon society during late-Georgian times.

Working Women of Somerset (£9.99) as told to James Crowden with photographs by Pauline Rook. Thirty Somerset women employed in a fascinating variety of occupations describe their working lives in their own words. Tales of hard work and achievement are accompanied by atmospheric black and white photographic portraits that give a remarkable insight into a rural community.

To find out more about Agre you can write to Agre Books, Groom's Cottage, Nettlecombe, Bridport, Dorset, DT6 3SS. You can read extracts from books and discover more about Agre's authors by visiting the website at www.agrebooks.co.uk.

'Comes' on old dear and have a corner of my pasty'